Cornell University Press, Est. 1869

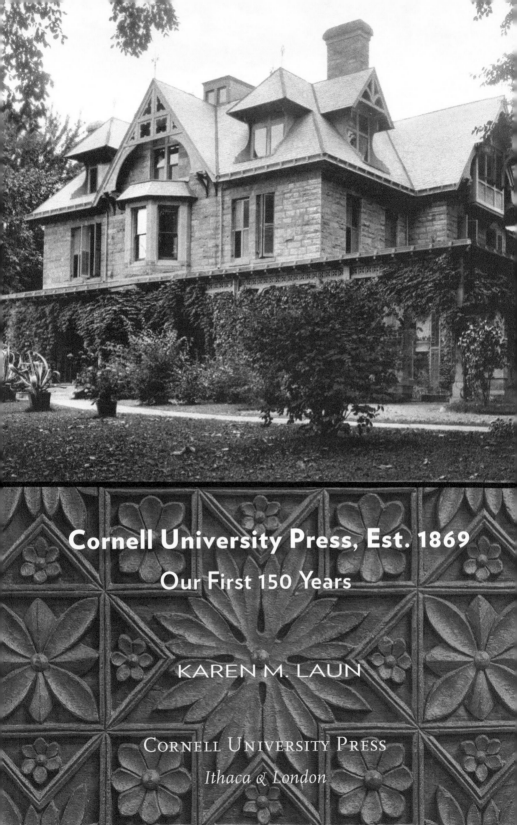

Cornell University Press, Est. 1869

Our First 150 Years

KAREN M. LAUN

CORNELL UNIVERSITY PRESS

Ithaca & London

The uncaptioned photos and decorative elements used in this book are architectural features found in historic Sage House, the home of Cornell University Press.

First published 2019 by Cornell University Press

Library of Congress Cataloging-in-Publication Data

Names: Laun, Karen M., 1970– author. | Cornell University Press, honouree.
Title: Cornell University Press, est. 1869 : our fi rst 150 years / Karen M. Laun.
Other titles: Cornell University Press, established 1869
Description: Ithaca [New York] : Cornell University Press, 2019. | Includes
bibliographical references.
Identifi ers: LCCN 2018052942 (print) | LCCN 2018053640 (ebook) |
ISBN 9781501740312 (pdf) | ISBN 9781501741258 (epub/mobi) |
ISBN 9781501740305 | ISBN 9781501740305 (pbk.)
Subjects: LCSH: Cornell University Press—History. | University presses—
New York (State)—Ithaca—History. | Scholarly publishing—New York
(State)—Ithaca—History.
Classification: LCC Z473.C765 (ebook) | LCC Z473.C765 L38 2019 (print) |
DDC 070.5/940974771—dc23
LC record available at https://lccn.loc.gov/2018052942

Contents

From Morse Code to Metadata: Bringing Scholarship to the World

Dean J. Smith

Director of Cornell University Press

As the thirteenth director of Cornell University Press since 1869, I arrive each morning acutely aware of my place in the continuum of this outstanding institution—the first of its kind in the nation. My current position reaches back in a direct line to Andrew Dickson White, who helped found the university and identified the need for a press to serve as an "intellectual organ" that would provide a publication outlet for scholarly achievements. White arranged the donation of a steam-driven cylinder press and type—our technology has fortunately advanced significantly since then. Since joining the press in 2015, I have focused my efforts on enabling the global access to and discovery of our high-quality humanities and social sciences scholarship, fulfilling the land-grant mission of Cornell University by demonstrating openness, promoting public accessibility, and disseminating knowledge that shapes the future of the world.

My office is just inside the mammoth front doors of Sage House, now a scholarly oasis on a terraced hillside halfway down East State Street. Cornell trustee Henry W. Sage built the house as his home and we now meet to discuss projects in the former dining room where he, President A. D. White, and the other members of the board of trustees discussed the future of the university. Sage House was later the Cornell Infirmary. Vestiges of the X-ray equipment remain visible on the conference room ceiling and this gives the press its modern day bona fides as a laboratory for experimentation and innovation.

On a shelf next to my desk rests a formidable corduroy ledger that tracked every expenditure from 1930 to the 1950s in handwritten columns. The production costs for our best-selling title, *The Handbook of Nature-Study* by Anna Botsford Comstock, were adroitly captured. The royalties for Linus Pauling's *The Nature of the Chemical Bond* totaled more than

$30,000 in the 1950s. Copies of correspondence from Vladimir Nabokov to former director Victor Reynolds are tucked between the pages. Throughout our history, we've published thousands of award-winning books and launched numerous careers. The history of the press is palpable to the touch.

The press is thriving in 2019. Our annual scholarly output is currently the highest in the press's history at 150 new titles per year. Our entire publication output—nearly 7,000 titles—is in the process of being digitized. We serve the *academy* as a credentialing body supporting the tenure process for thousands of scholars since our inception. We are aligned with the *university,* publishing faculty and Cornellians such as former president Frank H. T. Rhodes, ILR professor Samuel Bacharach, and the poet A. R. Ammons. We support the *community* through the publication of field guides and practical scientific research in books like *The Beekeeper's Handbook.* We provide visibility and access to our titles throughout the world via open access and digital collections. In an era of so-called fake news, the press is an authoritative voice. From the UN's role in covering up the cholera epidemic in Haiti (*Deadly River*), to a never-before-reported Bosnian genocide (*Violence as a Generative Force*), to a journalist's undercover view of a fascist group in Italy (*Sacrifice*), we take seriously our vision to change the world one book at a time.

I often reflect on university founder Ezra Cornell, who passionately pursued the idea of connecting communities through the telegraph, creating a vast network of communication. Samuel F. B. Morse hired Cornell to lay the cable for the test line because he had designed the machine to dig the trench. Publishing ground-breaking works requires an in-the-trenches mindset. As we enter our anniversary year, our publications are reaching communities in 150 countries. University presses like ours actively engage in ideas and solutions for making the world a better place through scholarship. Our classic titles can now engage new generations of scholars around the world. Our new books will reach a global audience through the discoverability and accessibility of the digital age. We refer to these activities as "Cornell Open."

We begin our next 150 years with a commitment to openness and inclusion. A. D. White's vision for the diffusion of learning and Ezra Cornell's advocacy for making higher education available to all gave rise to a university press. Our efforts to bring scholarship to the world extend the mission of Cornell University—that any person interested in any course of study can discover the scholarship contained within our publications. White's steam-driven press is long gone but our insightful forebears would most emphatically support and embrace our efforts today. Imagine a world in which university presses play a lead role in extending their university's brand on a global scale through the release of openly accessible monographs. It's already happening.

A Virtuous Circle of Scholarship

Gerald Beasley
Carl A. Kroch University Librarian

If I read three books every week this year, all published by Cornell University Press, I will keep up with its current rate of production. But I will still be leaving untouched its legacy of nearly 7,000 titles published over the last 150 years.

Cornell University Library has always had a strong relationship with Cornell University Press. As you will read in Karen Laun's excellent history, in 1869 Daniel Willard Fiske was the first university librarian as well as the first director of the press. He was also a professor of North European languages and established by bequest a series published by Cornell relating to Iceland and the Icelandic Collection he had founded. Its latest volume, *Islandica* 59 (2016), can be purchased in print from the press or downloaded free of charge from the library's online institutional repository, eCommons. Perhaps like me you are unsure which format you would prefer but grateful that you have a choice.

Much has changed and much has stayed the same at Cornell since 1869. The title of university librarian is now named in honor of Carl A. Kroch, a legendary bookseller, library supporter, and Cornell alumnus, who died in 1999. I was appointed Carl A. Kroch University Librarian in August 2017 and inherited the press from the vice provost for international affairs on January 1, 2018. I think press director Dean Smith's new reporting relationship to me suits us both very well. Certainly, academic libraries have always depended heavily on the expertise and output of university presses. Not only do the latter provide much of the content that libraries then make available, but their work also guides an understanding of what is attracting the attention of experts within any particular discipline. This in turn inspires the library's collection development initiatives. Hopefully the authors in question have found useful material for their research in libraries and archives. In any case, the virtuous circle is complete when an author's study is acquired by the library and itself becomes the source for new scholarship.

There are many other reasons why the anniversary of Cornell University Press should be celebrated. One is reputation. It is not easy to identify reliable knowledge by searching for it in the wide world of the web. A book from CUP, on the other hand, has undergone a rigorous process of review before it ever arrives in your hand or on your device. It is a quality product. Thanks to its reputation, built over a century and a half, you know a lot about its contents even before you begin reading. In a world increasingly vulnerable to half-truths and misinformation, that in itself is surely worth celebrating.

Cornell University Press, Est. 1869

A History of Cornell University Press (On the Occasion of Its Sesquicentennial Celebration)

In 1869, Ithaca, New York, was a thriving manufacturing town of about eight thousand inhabitants, though it was also still a place of dirt roads and outdoor privies, with only one train arriving per day. Up on East Hill, the fledgling Cornell University had been inaugurated just one year prior. The scattering of buildings on campus was surrounded by cow pasture, rambling fences, and rough roads; the several hundred students and professors lived and worked in spartan conditions. But the founders of Cornell, Ezra Cornell and Andrew Dickson White, had ambitious and innovative plans from the very start: a university where poorer students could pay their tuition through labor, where practical study was ranked equally with the classics, where women and African Americans could also earn a degree, and where a university press would be established—the first university press in the United States.

But like many claims of historic firsts—it's complicated. Cornell was not the first American university to have a printing press on campus. As early as 1640, Harvard College in Cambridge, Massachusetts, had a press that operated out of the president's house, but it was not officially associated with the college. Cornell's press was to be controlled entirely by the university. Cornell also cannot claim to have the oldest continuously operating press. That honor goes to Johns Hopkins University Press, founded in 1878. Cornell's press suffered financially and closed in 1884, not to reopen for nearly fifty years.

The fact remains, however, that the founders of Cornell understood the importance of a university press in fulfilling the university's mission: to disseminate knowledge, to educate citizens, and to promote a culture of inquiry. And 150 years later, the story of Cornell University Press, because of (rather than in spite of) its caveats and asterisks, is far more remarkable than merely one of being "the first."

Early press logo

First Edition: America's First University Press

If there is a theme that runs throughout the history of scholarly publishing in the United States it is the constant tension between fulfilling a mission and finding sufficient resources to do so. Creating a university press at Cornell was a vital part of President A. D. White's educational ideas. He envisioned a press on the European model—controlled by the university and with the goal of the diffusion of new learning. It was not to be the kind of university press we see today, acquiring and editing scholarly works from around the world. Instead it was to be a print shop, dedicated to printing and distributing texts associated with the university administration, faculty, and students. From the very beginning, however, there was some resistance from the trustees, who did not see running a printing press as a legitimate part of the university's business. At the seventh board of trustees meeting, in February 1868, a committee comprising three New York politicians and newspaper editors, Erastus Brooks, George H. Andrews, and Horace Greeley, founder of the *New-York Tribune*, was appointed to determine the "practicability and desirability" of a University Printing House.

Ezra Cornell, founder of Cornell University, 1868

Andrew Dickson White, founder and president of Cornell University, 1878

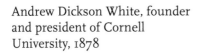

It is here that the ideas of the practical Ezra Cornell come in. In keeping with a key part of his famous saying, "I would found an institution where any person can find instruction in any study," the founders intended to make higher education accessible to those students who had merit, but lacked the funds to pay tuition. In its earliest years, Cornell University included a labor corps where students helped erect university buildings, worked on the farm or in the machine shop, and constructed roads. Included in this ambitious concept was the university press. The labor corps was not intended as an apprenticeship;

students were expected to have experience and for their labor to benefit the university as well as themselves.

The press is not mentioned again in the trustees' notes until June 1869 when the board of trustees appointed Daniel Willard Fiske as the first director. White and Fiske had been friends since boyhood, and Fiske was an important adviser to White in the early stages of planning the university. Fiske's background was well suited to running the press. He had already been appointed the university librarian, held a chair in North European languages, and had been an editor of the *Hartford Courant* in Connecticut.

In those early days, the press, lacking any substantial monetary support allocated by the trustees, was fortunate to benefit from the goodwill of university supporters. An October 1869 letter from R. Hoe and Company of New York City to A. D. White reveals that a large Hoe printing press, valued at $2,500, had been sent via railway as a gift to the university. George Bruce's Son and Company sent $400 worth of type. The board of trustees allocated $300 for additional purchases and Willard Fiske ordered more type from White's New York Type Foundry, including Greek lettering.

Daniel Willard Fiske, first director of the press, 1880

Though not yet adequately supplied, the press also needed the people to run it. Willard Fiske oversaw the operation of the press, but the day-to-day work required different skills. It is no coincidence that the press was founded in connection with the College of the Mechanic Arts—this was complex machinery and dirty, ink-stained work. The man found to manage the press was B. Hermon Smith, an experienced printer who had worked for the *Syracuse Journal* and had his own print shop in Syracuse. An ad in the 1868–69 gazetteer and business directory for Onondaga County describes Smith (or rather, he most likely describes himself) as "a young man of great energy, a thorough mechanic and bred to the printing business . . . a neat and tasty printer." Smith was dedicated to the success of the university press from the start and offered to borrow $3,000 on his own account for the purchase of a second (Gordon) press and additional material.

The new enterprise was set up in the basement of Morrill Hall, with an attached shed for the steam power to operate the Hoe press. It provided employment for twenty students, many of them in the civil engineering field. Students worked four hours each afternoon, all day on Saturday, and "during the whole available time in vacation," according to George Lincoln Burr '81, a Cornell professor and former student employee.

Morrill Hall, the first home of the press, 1868

One of the first publications was the *Cornell Register*, an annual listing of students, faculty, courses, and entrance exam requirements that the press printed for several years. On the back page of the 1869–70 edition is the earliest known advertisement for the press, clearly laying out its alignment with Ezra Cornell's vision of the university: "Its employees are all young men, who are endeavoring, by means of their own labor, to defray the expenses of a University education."

THE UNIVERSITY PRESS, *one of the industrial establishments founded in connection* with the COLLEGE OF THE MECHANIC ARTS, *in the Cornell University, is completely furnished with all the requirements of a* FIRST CLASS PRINTING OFFICE, *including Hoe and Gordon Steam Presses, and every Variety of Type, Ink and Paper, American and English. Its foremen, compositors, pressmen and engineer, are all Matriculated Students of the University.* THE UNIVERSITY PRESS *is especially prepared to do book or pamphlet work of every description and in every style. It solicits the patronage of the public for two reasons:* — First. *It attempts to do its work well;* Second. *Its employees are all young men, who are endeavoring, by means of their own labor, to defray the expenses of a University education.*

The first known advertisement by the press, *Cornell Register*, 1869

A later director of the press, Woodford Patterson '95, related a story in which George Lincoln Burr's father wrote to A. D. White asking how his son might work his way through school. White advised that he learn the printer's trade. The younger Burr did just that, working at the *Cortland Standard* until he was ready for college. Burr then worked at the press from 1877 to 1879, later becoming White's private secretary, the curator and cataloguer of the historical library White was gathering, and a much-admired professor of ancient and medieval history at Cornell.

Most of the names of early press employees are lost to time, but the students, despite their busy class and work schedules, did manage to form a university press baseball team. The *Cornell Era* reported that the lineup for 1870 included G. Whitfield Farnham, captain and head of the book department, Charles Spencer Francis, catcher and future ambassador to Austria-Hungary, and Abraham Gridley, third base and a future lawyer in Penn Yan.

George Lincoln Burr, Cornell professor and early student employee of the press

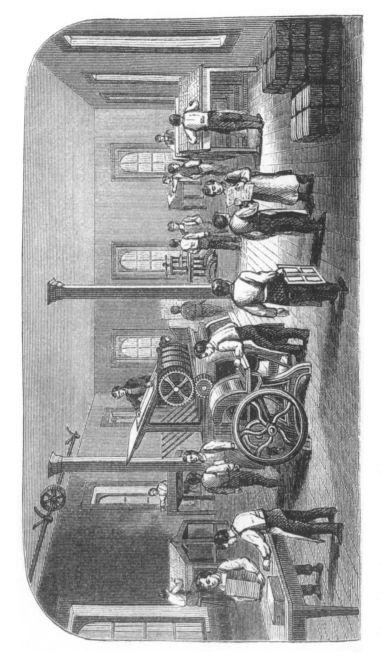

The earliest known image of the press. Engraving in *Scribner's Monthly* (May 1873)

In 1871, the press moved to a large, well-lit room in the newly built Sibley College of the Mechanic Arts (the western wing of the present Sibley building). The large Hoe printing press was powered by a turbine wheel far below in Fall Creek and a stereotype foundry was added in the rear of the building around 1874. An article about Cornell University in the May 1873 edition of *Scribner's Monthly* included an engraving of the new quarters, the earliest known image of the press. The one man wearing a coat, standing on the Hoe press, may well be a depiction of B. Hermon Smith, who had been appointed director in 1871.

The second home of the press in the west wing of Sibley College, 1872

Cornell students in those early years were generally considered well behaved, but were not above occasional mischief. In 1871, Smith wrote a strongly worded letter to the *Cornell Era* expressing his "detestation of the manner in which some of the students conduct themselves, when visiting the office of the University Press. They seem to hold to the belief that the fixtures and machinery of the office are public property—that every wheel is for them to turn, every page and case of type for them to pi, and worse than all else, every piece of manuscript for them to read." He welcomed polite visitors but "loungers" must keep out and he hoped that such people would remember "the next thing in order after a *hint*."

When not dealing with the hijinks of students, Smith initiated a change at the press that reflected the innovative nature of the university—hiring women to set type. An October 1872 note in the *Daily Journal* of Ithaca mentions that Smith had hired "lady compositors" and had also written an article for the Syracuse *Typo* on the topic.

In 1874, Smith added to his duties by teaching a class in typography as part of a new journalism course. Fiske saw a need for well-educated and well-trained journalists who also had experience in typesetting and proofreading. The journalism course was offered for only four years and just one student was awarded the "licentiate in Journalism," in 1876.

Throughout these years, the press produced an impressive number of publications. Not all of these are known due to their ephemeral nature—syllabi, lecture notes, short-lived student publications, and the like. There were few books of a learned nature, although that was one of A. D. White's initial goals. Instead, the press served primarily as a printing office for the routine publication needs of faculty and students, in addition to taking on work for outside publishers.

The press did endeavor to publish works of scholarship by Cornell faculty. They began a series (that ultimately consisted of only two volumes) titled *Bulletin of the Cornell University: Science*. These two pamphlets, published in 1874, dealt with a scientific expedition to Brazil by two instructors. In 1872, the press also published *The Cornell University: What It Is and What It Is Not*, A. D. White's proud defense of Cornell University against criticisms for being nondenominational and allowing students to choose their own course of study.

In addition to printing the annual editions of the *Cornell Register* from 1869 to 1875, the press published an account of the 1869 university inauguration, various laws and documents of the university, outlines for lectures by White and other professors, and, in 1878, the *Ten-Year Book of the Cornell University*—an alumni directory.

Student publications included the weekly newspaper the *Cornell Era*, printed by the press from 1869 to 1873, the *Aurora Brasiliera*, a monthly published by the Brazilian students in 1873 and 1874, and *Cocagne*, an early attempt at collegiate humor that had six issues in 1878. The press also did work for outside publishers and printed one or more books on North American ethnology by the noted anthropologist Lewis Henry Morgan for Henry Holt & Co. of New York. Ithaca's *Daily Journal* reported in July 1877 that eight compositors were working to make the forms for plates to be cast in the stereotype foundry, up to 162 plates in a single day. They were doing work for Henry Holt and for William F. Gill & Co. of Boston, who had ordered a large, heavily illustrated volume of Tennyson's complete works.

Despite the number of publications, it seems that the press was never financially successful. *Landmarks of Tompkins County*, published in 1894, indicated a yearly deficit that had to be made good by the university treasury. According to Woodford Patterson, all of the university's official print-ing had been promised to the press in consideration of B. Hermon Smith's personal investment in the business, but the volume of work appeared to have exceeded the capacity of the shop. The press had the potential to be profitable if it could but obtain more investment from the trustees. By the late 1870s, however, the university was undergoing difficul-ties of its own, in part from the absence of its leader's guiding hand. President White had taken a two-year European sabbat-ical for his health and upon his return in 1879 was offered the position of American minister to Germany. When his resig-nation from the university was refused, he took another leave of absence in order to accept the position. In addition, money was tight due to a dwindling endowment, and enrollment dropped from 542 in 1876 to 384 in 1881 as tuition rose and opportunities to be self-supporting through the labor corps declined. The travails of the university press were not the highest priority for the trustees.

White returned to Ithaca and the presidency in 1881, but despite his efforts it was by then too late for the press. In 1882, the board of trustees resolved that the press be abol-ished, though the matter was tabled at the time. President White's annual report in 1883 asked for additional investment in the press and bemoaned that while it had done much work "and has done it well; . . . it cannot with its present means and accommodations render the service that we might easily secure from it." After the death of Ezra Cornell in 1874, the stu-dent labor corps, never particularly successful, no longer had a champion to promote it and faded away. The most successful aspect of the labor corps, as well as the best way to honor that part of the founder's vision, asserted White, was the univer-sity press, which had produced a "considerable number of the best students we have ever had . . . support[ing] themselves mainly or entirely" by working at the press. (White was likely thinking of George Lincoln Burr, whom White described as one of the two geniuses who attended Cornell during his presidency.)

President White's next report, issued in June 1884, lamented that the press had been discontinued the previous term, costing the university the ability to securely print examination papers or complex projects that local printers in Ithaca could not manage. The director, Smith, had left the press and taken the equipment he had provided with him, as the executive committee was unwilling to purchase it. White expressed his hope that the press would be reestablished "at some day not distant."

White did make an attempt to keep the press going, mentioning in the same report and one the following year that an unnamed head of a college printing house, who sought more opportunity, was willing to invest his own capital if the university would match the amount and pay him a fair salary. The candidate, Gustave Weinschenk of Harvard, whose name was revealed in the local paper, came to town to discuss the possibility, but the university trustees were apparently unwilling to meet his demands as nothing came of the proposal.

Over the next few years, no great efforts were made to revive the press and White had already acknowledged in 1885 that providing for Sibley College and the veterinary clinic took priority. In 1887, the trustees approved a contract with Walter G. Smith & Co. to rent part of Sibley and use the presses, but it must have fallen through as there is no record of income. According to Woodford Patterson, equipment was moved into storage, some of it was sold, and some rusted and was discarded. The type and type cases went to a local printer, Andrus & Church, to be used only for Cornell work.

After a short fifteen years, the first run of Cornell University Press had come to an end. A line in *Landmarks of Tompkins County* attempted to put a full stop to the story, stating flatly that "this experiment demonstrated . . . that material profit was impossible in philanthropy." The absence of a press did not, however, erase the existence of President White's mission—there was still a desire and a need for meritorious scholarship to be published and disseminated to students, to academics, and to the broader public. What happened next is perhaps the most remarkable part of the story of Cornell University Press. Over the next four and a half decades, it was the dedicated efforts of faculty, students, and alumni who kept the idea of a university press at Cornell alive, and who gradually laid the groundwork for its rebirth.

Early press logo

Revisions: Comstock Publishing and the Long Campaign to Reestablish the Press

After the closure of the university press in 1884, scholarly publishing at Cornell continued, although the work was outsourced to MacMillan, Ginn & Co., and Yale University Press. In 1887, the first volume of Cornell Studies in Classical Philology was published, followed by Cornell Studies of Philosophy in 1900 and Cornell Studies in English in 1917. The university also maintained the position of university publisher, and from 1917 until his retirement this position was held by Woodford Patterson, also the first director of the press when it reopened.

The university library undertook publishing ventures as well, including a catalogue of the Dante collection in 1898 and then the long-running Islandica series in 1908. Established through a bequest from Willard Fiske, this series has produced fifty-nine volumes relating to Iceland and Fiske's collection of Icelandic literature as of 2016, with many of the later issues published by the press.

The most significant development in publishing at Cornell during this time period was initiated by two Cornell professors and former Cornell students, John Henry Comstock '74 and Simon Henry Gage '77. Comstock had come to Cornell to study entomology, but the lack of appropriate courses forced him to devise his own course of study. He was so successful that, in his sophomore year, his fellow students petitioned that he be given the opportunity to teach a course for credit. Comstock went on to establish the first department of entomology in the United States, making it a world center for entomological study. When not engaged in his studies, he also served as caretaker of Touchdown, Cornell's bear mascot, and chimes master in McGraw Tower.

Gage studied medicine, originally planning to become a physician. Like Comstock, he taught biology classes while still an undergraduate and after graduation became a professor of comparative anatomy, histology, and embryology, as well as an important figure in the history of American microscopy.

John Henry Comstock, founder of Comstock Publishing, late 1800s

Simon Henry Gage, founder of Comstock Publishing, 1903

Both men studied under and assisted Burt Green Wilder, a former Civil War surgeon and professor of comparative anatomy and natural history, who had been appointed in 1867 and spent his entire academic career at Cornell. He was a legendary figure on campus—his energetic lectures, dedicated efforts to obtain exotic specimens for dissections, and many personal quirks well documented in Morris Bishop's *A History of Cornell.*

According to an unpublished 1944 history of Comstock Publishing by Simon Gage and Clara Starrett Gage, there were few published guides for laboratory work in natural history in the 1870s and the university encouraged its teachers to produce such guides for their students. John Comstock published *Notes on Entomology* in 1876—printed by the original Cornell University Press. The first four editions of Gage's landmark work, *The Microscope,* were printed by Andrus & Church in Ithaca. These early publications were made solely for the use of Cornell students and either donated to them or sold at a nominal cost. The need for useful and practical scientific guides, made affordable for students on a tight budget, played a key role in influencing Comstock's and Gage's next venture.

In 1892, one year before the twenty-fifth anniversary of Cornell's founding, Comstock and Gage decided to honor Wilder, their former professor and mentor, and conceived the idea of publishing a Festschrift—a congratulatory volume of essays of original research by his former students and the first volume of its kind published in the United States. For this purpose, they formed the Comstock Publishing Company and produced *The Wilder Quarter Century Book* in 1893, the first book to bear the Comstock imprint.

With a publishing company thus established, Comstock and Gage decided to bring out their future guides and textbooks under the Comstock imprint. The next book to be published was the fifth edition of *The Microscope* in 1894, soon followed in 1895 by *A Manual for the Study of Insects*, by Comstock and his wife, Anna Botsford Comstock '85.

As before, the purpose of publishing these books was solely for the benefit of Cornell students. It turned out, however, that when students graduated they took the books with them for further use, and teachers at other institutions began to adopt them as well. In time, Comstock and Gage found themselves running a genuine publishing business and they set out two principles to guide their work: 1) excellence in printing and binding (in part to best display the fine wood engravings created by Anna Botsford Comstock) and 2) affordability of the volumes for both teachers and students (at the time, half or less than what was charged for similar publications). Because the founders did all of the writing of the early publications and ran the business out of the Comstock household, they were able to keep expenses low. Defying expectations and the earlier example of the university press, they made publishing with a mission profitable.

In the early 1900s, Comstock Publishing expanded to include works by authors other than the founders—the first single-authored title was by James G. Needham '98, Cornell professor of limnology (the study of inland waters). And it was around this time that Anna Botsford Comstock began to play an even larger role in the company's success. Up to this point she had coauthored books with her husband, but now forged her own path with her involvement in the nature study movement.

Anna Botsford Comstock, though not one of the principals of the company at the time of its founding, was a remarkable figure in the history of Cornell in her own right and as vital for Comstock Publishing's success as her husband and Gage. Anna Botsford entered Cornell in 1874 with the intent

Anna Botsford Comstock, author, illustrator, and a leader of the nature study movement

of studying science and nature. She met John Comstock when she was a student in one of his lectures; they married in 1878 and she later finished her studies in 1885, graduating with a degree in natural history. Throughout her life she supported her husband's work by supplying finely detailed illustrations for his research. She was also the first female professor at Cornell in 1898 (though she was denied full professorship until 1920) and, in 1923, was chosen by the League of Women Voters as one of the twelve greatest living American women to have "contributed most in their respective fields for the betterment of the world."

The nature study movement emerged after the depression of 1893, which drove families off farms in search of factory work in urban areas. A concern rose that rural areas and farming would decline if children did not grow up immersed in and understanding the natural world and farming life. Cornell was a leader in the nature study movement, beginning with extension courses in Chautauqua County. The mantra of this movement, "study nature, not books," is reflected, in a modified form that embraces Comstock's publishing mission, in the motto once prominently displayed on the chalet where the business was housed: "Through books to nature."

In 1896, Liberty Hyde Bailey, the well-known American horticulturist and teacher of plant science at Cornell, placed Anna Comstock in charge of building interest in nature study in New York's rural schools. She began a long crusade of visiting schools, lecturing, and writing educational pamphlets, then gathered the results of her work to write what became the teacher's bible for nature study, *The Handbook of Nature-Study*. In her recollections she wrote that she conceived of the idea of the book in 1909 but that no one supported it, even her own husband, who felt that the book would never pay for the printing. Anna Comstock disagreed strongly and "went at [her] task with teeth set and defiant courage." When the *Handbook* was published in 1911 it was not only financially successful but was soon considered the most important book of Comstock Publishing, still in print today in its twenty-fourth edition.

Additional nature study publications at this time included books for use by pupils in schools or at summer camps. The *Field and Camp Notebook* took the form of a slim loose-leaf binder containing a selection of pages on birds, ferns, trees, insects, stars, and many other subjects, accompanied by delicately rendered drawings of birds and animals by Louis Agassiz Fuertes '97, an Ithaca native and renowned ornithologist and artist. After Liberty Hyde Bailey founded the American Nature-Study Society in 1908, the organization's journal, *The Nature-Study Review*, was published by Comstock Publishing and edited by Anna Comstock until 1923.

As Comstock Publishing grew, it expanded not only its partnership (with Anna Comstock and James G. Needham brought on as co-owners) but its offices. Originally housed in an annex to the campus Insectary, it moved in 1911 to the basement of the Comstock's new home at 123 Roberts Place. An additional staff member, William A. Slingerland, was brought on to handle administrative matters. Comstock Publishing had grown from a one-off idea to publish a commemorative book to a full-fledged and prosperous publishing concern.

The partners soon realized the need for a fireproof building to protect all their drawings, engravings, woodcuts, and printed material so, in 1914, a piece of land opposite the Comstock home was purchased for a new building. A Swiss chalet (124 Roberts Place), designed by Arthur Norman Gibbs '90, was built with the basement and first floor largely reserved for the publishing work and the second floor designed as living quarters. Alfred Marshak '30, reminisced in a letter to the

Bird drawings by Louis Agassiz Fuertes for the
Field and Camp Notebook

Cornell Plantations magazine that he had lived in "the Chalet" as a student and nearly flooded the basement storeroom when he forgot to turn off a valve on the coal furnace he was responsible for tending. Gage, fortunately, came to the rescue before any books were damaged.

Comstock Publishing continued to prosper but its founders were aging, turning more and more of the management, particularly of the loose-leaf notebooks business, over to Slingerland. There was some question about his ability to properly manage the company and legal action was taken to dispute the distribution of profits between himself and the Comstocks, eventually resulting in Slingerland's separation from the business. In 1926, John Comstock became ill and his health deteriorated over the next five years. Anna Comstock passed away in 1930, followed by her husband in 1931.

According to the Comstocks' wills, the bulk of their estate, including their interests in Comstock Publishing, was bequeathed to Cornell University. This included the Chalet, with the desire that it should remain the home of Comstock Publishing. Simon Gage also transferred his rights to the company to the university. With two of the driving forces behind Comstock Publishing gone, the future of the company was in flux, but the generosity of the Comstocks and Gage would become a key element in the revival and success of Cornell University Press.

Another crucial development was the growing chorus of voices declaring that Cornell needed a university press. Members of the faculty, students, and alumni lobbied for decades for its reestablishment and devised various plans for

The chalet at Roberts Place, home of Comstock Publishing, sometime between 1915 and 1930

funding. In 1909, the student publication the *Cornell Era* ran a short unsigned article, "Cornell Needs a Press," imagining it still as a print shop. In May 1916, Lane Cooper, professor of English language and literature, editor of the Cornell Studies in English series, future press author, and one of the most dedicated advocates for reopening the press, wrote a lengthy editorial on this subject in the *Cornell Alumni News*. Written prior to the US entry into World War I, he lamented the loss of European students and professors to the battlefield and the dwindling publication of scholarship overseas, but argued that this brought opportunity and responsibility to Cornell if "some man of wealth be induced to endow a press." In his vision, he imagined a press for the whole nation, publishing works of the highest merit from any university.

Lane Cooper, Cornell professor and press advocate

In 1918, the student humor publication the *Cornell Widow* voted to give up half its profits for the establishment of a university press. This generous offer was a bit empty, however, as their profits had vanished after the United States began sending soldiers, including over 4,500 commissioned officers from Cornell, to fight in World War I. President Jacob Gould Schurman promoted the idea of an endowed press as an important element of a complete university. In his 1918–19 annual report he wrote that "productive scholarship thrives where scholars enjoy free interchange of thought with the world of scholars. Isolated from the world, it withers." It was the press, he added, that was the best channel for this interchange.

The calls for a university press grew more demanding in the 1920s, frequently acknowledging that a press would likely not be profitable but that its work was vital. An unsigned editorial in the *Daily Sun*, written as President Livingston Farrand prepared to be inaugurated in 1921, stated that "the most valuable books intellectually are frequently the least valuable commercially," but that "research is one of the vital functions of a university, and its results one of the university's greatest contributions to civilization." Lane Cooper (who would go on to publish fifteen books with the press) reemerged in 1923, writing in the *Daily Sun* that "the work of the university press would be like that of the University Library. The Library is not a paying concern, yet it is the most valuable and useful part of Cornell University; and it owes its excellence . . . to the far-sighted persons who endowed it."

By the end of the 1920s there was impatience but also signs of optimism among the press's advocates. The writer of an unsigned editorial in the *Daily Sun* (1927) criticized how little had been accomplished other than research about other presses, but felt it likely that a press "will be established at Cornell to herald a real awakening on the part of the whole

University to its opportunity to disseminate knowledge far beyond its own walls." Another *Daily Sun* editorial (1929) about the allocation of alumni donations declared "we should be delighted to sacrifice a few halfbacks for the success of so laudable an enterprise."

Then came the turning point. The years of stating and restating the case for having a university press at Cornell, the Comstocks' bequests to the university, and, strangely, the start of the Great Depression all combined to create the perfect conditions for reopening Cornell University Press and bringing back to life this part of A. D. White's original educational mission. As the unknown editorialist wrote in the *Daily Sun*, it was a "matter of pride that the literary fruits of Cornell be presented to the world by Cornell."

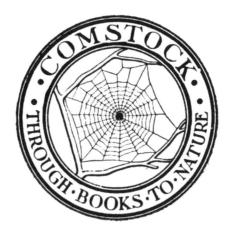

Early Comstock logo. The spider web was drawn by Anna Botsford Comstock.

Second Edition: "University Press Redivivus"

B etween 1929 and 1931, when all the pieces moved into place for what Morris Bishop called the University Press Redivivus—the university press reborn—a key figure who emerged was Woodford Patterson '95, the university publisher and secretary of the university. Patterson, a Newark Valley native, had worked for the *New York Evening Sun* and served as editor for the *Cornell Alumni News*. He cared deeply about the art of bookmaking, later designing many books for the press. A gift he left behind, recently rediscovered in the back of a closet at Sage House, was a collection of several dozen of his own books, meant to serve as examples of good book design. Many contain brief notes attached inside the front covers, extoling the use of particular ligatures, generous margins, or marginal subheads.

One of these books, a history of Oxford University Press, also includes a handwritten account from Patterson of how the Wall Street Crash of 1929 led to President Farrand's recommendation that the press be reopened. The economic hardships precipitated the decision of Longmans, Green & Company to cancel their contracts for the listing and sale of two Cornell Studies series, Philosophy and Classical Philology. In 1930, on Patterson's request, Farrand persuaded the trustees to set up a new Cornell University Press, which would be under Patterson's management and handle all university publishing previously conducted by outside agencies. This included the two series at Longmans, the Cornell Studies in English series, the Baker Lectures in Chemistry, and the university library publications. Storage space was found in Morrill Hall and Patterson agreed to handle orders, shipments, and the publication of an annual catalogue.

The press was officially reestablished at the June 1930 board of trustees meeting and allocated a subsidy of $5,000 per year from the alumni fund for a period of five years. The writer of an editorial in the *Cornell Daily Sun* considered this a meager amount but a good step forward. The following year, when the ownership of Comstock Publishing was transferred to the university, the press's chances for success were further increased.

The reorganized Comstock Publishing was incorporated in 1931, with Gage as president and Woodford Patterson as general manager. At the board of trustees meeting in June 1931, the net profits of Comstock Publishing were dedicated to the support of the university press so that the funds would be used solely for publishing scholarly works and not absorbed into the general university budget. At the same meeting, it was determined that the press should also be housed in the Chalet and its business operations managed by Comstock. In this way, the newly reborn university press was kept under the protective wing of Comstock Publishing. They were separate entities, but shared space, staff, and expenses.

The press also benefited from the income of an established backlist from the Cornell Studies series and the library publications, some sixty titles in all. The goal was to eventually publish additional works of scholarship and scientific research by Cornell faculty. Probably the most notable press publication of this first decade was Nobel Prize–winner Linus Pauling's

Nature of the Chemical Bond, part of the Baker lecture series, while Comstock published the first edition of H. H. Dukes's *Physiology of Domestic Animals*, a classic in veterinary studies, and the *Handbook of Frogs and Toads*, by Anna Allen Wright and Albert Hazen Wright.

By 1938, the management of two independent but intertwined publishing concerns was becoming unwieldy. Comstock Publishing was providing the press with office space, storage, shipping facilities, and business management, in addition to handing over all its profits. But oversight from the university was different for each, with the press reporting to a Committee on Publication and a University Press Council, while Comstock reported solely to its directors. A committee formed by President Edmund Ezra Day proposed that the operation of the university press be managed by a board of directors and a board of editors. The directors were to be the same directors who oversaw Comstock, while the editors would be the director of the press and four members of the faculty. And yet, despite sharing so many aspects of its business with the university press, it was not until 1951 that Comstock Publishing Company was officially liquidated as a corporation and redesignated as an imprint of Cornell University Press.

In 1940, Woodford Patterson retired as director of the press, though he remained as a consulting editor for several more years. Stanley Schaefer '28, who had come to work at Comstock Publishing as an undergraduate, moved from his position as the business manager of Comstock to the joint position of director of Comstock and the press. Schaefer then left in 1943 to become manager of production and head of the editorial offices at F. S. Crofts and Company of New York, publishers of college textbooks. He was replaced by Victor Reynolds, who had formerly worked at Macmillan Company as a promotion director, as well as at F. S. Crofts and Ronald

Press. During his twenty years at Cornell, Reynolds also served as president of the American Association of University Presses (AAUP, now AUPresses) from 1953 to 1955.

Woodford Patterson, press director
1930–1940

Stanley Schaefer, press director
1940–1943

Victor Reynolds, press director
1943–1963

By 1943, the publishing partnership had outgrown its offices. The upper floor of the Chalet had been rented to Simon Gage, who passed away in 1944, and the press moved into that space as well. By the end of the decade, the press also opened a warehouse in a Quonset hut in East Ithaca.

Employee stocking shelves in the press warehouse, 1950s or 1960s

During World War II, restrictions on the purchase of paper limited the publication of new books and editions, but Comstock and the press continued to grow in size and explore new publishing ideas. By 1944, the seventy-fifth anniversary of the founding of the press, the backlist had grown to 250 books, plus nineteen new publications that year. In 1948, Victor Reynolds estimated the press, with twenty-four new publications, to be among the top ten university presses in volume.

Authentic
Recordings
of Nature's
Amazing
Voices

Brochure advertising
Cornell Records, which
distributed recordings of
birds, frogs, and insects

In 1942, an innovative partnership began between Comstock and the Laboratory of Ornithology at Cornell, with Comstock distributing wildlife recordings. These eventually led to the formation of the Cornell Records Division, possibly the first record business among university presses. The first album was *American Bird Songs*, a six-record set, followed in 1948 by *Voices of the Night*, recordings of North American frogs and toads. Other recordings, ultimately twelve in all, included jungle sounds, western bird songs, and insect sounds.

The press also took over publication of four journals: *The Philosophical Review, Far Eastern Review, New York Folklore Quarterly*, and *Industrial and Labor Relations Review*. In addition, the press managed the printing of many official publications of the university and began a joint imprint with the New School for Social Research in New York City.

The 1950s were a time of great growth for Cornell University, with many new buildings and an increased focus on research. The press also continued its trend of growth and change. While the press largely published books by Cornell faculty through the 1930s and 1940s, this number gradually shrank to one-half or perhaps one-third of the annual list in the 1950s and even less in coming decades as the press began to solicit more work from other academic institutions. The press also expanded beyond its foundational science, history, and literary criticism and theory publications to explore topics of interest to the post-war world through two series on civil liberties and the development of western civilization, in addition to books on the Middle East and the Soviet Union. Important publications included *The Bill of Rights Reader* by Milton R. Konvitz, one of the founders of Cornell's School of Industrial and Labor Relations, and *The Middle East in World Affairs* by George Lenczowski.

In 1955, the press introduced another innovation in scholarly publishing, becoming the first university press to publish paperback books. Great Seal Books, named after the seal of the university, produced paperback reprints of classic works by leading scholars, continuing the joint press and Comstock mission of disseminating worthy scholarship at an affordable price. Selected from the fields of the humanities, sciences, and social sciences, these books included *The Rise of Universities* by Charles Homer Haskins, *Ethical Systems and Legal Ideals* by Felix S. Cohen, *Science and Imagination* by Marjorie Nicolson, and *Bees: Their Vision, Chemical Senses, and Language* by Karl von Frisch.

By the end of the 1950s, the press was publishing over thirty-five books a year and assisted with the editorial, design, and production needs of several journals: *Administrative Science Quarterly, The Cornell Veterinarian, The Federal Accountant, Rural Sociology,* and *Student Medicine.* Joint imprints were cultivated with the American Historical Association, the Folger Shakespeare Library, Amherst College, and the New York Historical Association. The press also sought to expand its global reach, becoming part of the International Book Export Group (IBEG) with the presses at Columbia, Harvard, Princeton, and Yale.

To accommodate the press's increase in publications, the number of staff had grown as well, creating space issues in the Chalet. Being a true Swiss chalet, it had always been an unusual place to work, with no interior stairs between the first and second floors. The publicity director's office was reached by a flight of attic stairs and the assistant director's office was surrounded by a balcony. When the press expanded to another chalet at 122 Roberts Place, staff members were even more scattered about—the director and several editors occupied offices in 122, the receptionist in 124, and, later, when the press had expanded into a third neighboring building (the former home of Leon Rothschild, owner of Rothschild's Department Store in Ithaca), the manuscript editing department was located in all three buildings. Adding to the list of the Chalet's quirks, Simon Gage left an instructional note for Victor Reynolds on which water taps to open and doors to leave ajar to avoid frozen pipes in the depths of winter.

Heading into the 1960s, the press experienced a record year of sales at a time of growth for university presses generally. The AAUP boasted fifty-three members and scholarly presses were publishing one out of every four books in the United States. A new organization formed at Cornell, the Prelis Cornelliensis Amici Fidelissimi, a group of all former and present members of the board of editors. The purpose was to meet annually to hear a progress report, and to discuss old times and new books. Sadly, this tongue twister of a club has not survived.

Roger Howley, press director 1963–1982

In 1963, Victor Reynolds resigned to become the first director of a new university press for the University of Virginia. He was replaced by Roger Howley '49, a native of the Ithaca area who had worked for Macmillan and Johns Hopkins University Press. In that same year Bernhard Kendler came to work at the press, first as managing editor but then as the first acquisitions editor. Prior to this time acquisitions had been handled by the directors. Over the next four decades, Kendler developed strong lists in classics, literature, and art history, in addition to building the press into the leading publisher of academic philosophy in English. He is remembered for his skill in acquiring the best books and developing authors into better writers. His quick wit is also still cherished, as well as preserved in memos in the press archives. A typical comment about a manuscript, delivered with his usual good humor, reads: "There's clearly still some pomposity, with jargonic interludes."

As the press approached the hundredth anniversary of its founding, it had grown to approximately forty employees and surpassed one million dollars in gross annual sales. Cornell Paperbacks (originally Great Seal Books) numbered forty-six titles and had sold nearly half a million copies. Between fifty and seventy-five new titles were published each year in subjects covering the range of the university curriculum and including monographs, translations, advanced reference books, and serious nonfiction written for scholars and general readers. The new anthropology list included Victor Turner's *Forest of Symbols*, and the new Cornell Publications in the History of Science series featured Henry Guerlac's *Lavoisier: The Crucial Year*. David Brion Davis's 1966 publication, *The Problem of Slavery in Western Culture*, was awarded the Pulitzer Prize in 1967. Other authors whose books had been published by the press since its revival represent some of the most distinguished names in American scholarship: Carl Becker, Max Black, Lane Cooper, Mario Einaudi, Walter Gellhorn, George Kahin, Milton Konvitz, Linus Pauling, Clinton Rossiter, and Moses Coit Tyler, the first professor of American history in the United States.

From left, Katherine Sturdevant (chief editor), John Wasner (production manager), Robert Clausen (author and Cornell professor of botany), and Evelyn Boyce (associate manuscript editor) review proof pages, 1961

In 1969, its anniversary year, the press hosted the annual AAUP conference. The main speaker at the banquet was Morris Bishop '13, Cornell professor of Romance literature, university historian, poet, and author of *A History of Cornell*, published by the press in 1962. Bishop spoke on "The Lower Depths of Higher Education," an amusing depiction of the imagined good old days of nineteenth-century university life that, in reality, were a time of physical hardship, frequent riots, and erratic education. It was a time of deep dissatisfaction with higher education that, though the written version of his speech does not explicitly do so, could be compared to the turbulent campus life of the 1960s. Bishop's speech was particularly timely as the conference was held just two months after the thirty-six-hour student takeover of Willard Straight Hall, where armed members of Cornell's Afro-American Society protested racial injustice and the university's slow progress in establishing a black studies program. Three decades later, the press published an in-depth exploration of these events in *Cornell '69: Liberalism and the Crisis of the American University* by Donald Alexander Downs.

In the 1970s, the press's activities took on an increasingly international dimension, copublishing books that originated with British publishers, up to fifteen titles per year, and frequently licensing publishers to sell translated editions of Cornell books. Together with Johns Hopkins University Press and the University of California Press, the press opened an office in London for easier sale and distribution of books in the United Kingdom, Europe, the Middle East, and Africa. By 1976, the press was publishing more than seventy books per year and selling more than a quarter million per year. The wide range of titles was particularly strong in the fields of history, literary criticism, philosophy, and Southeast Asian studies, in addition to the applied biology books of the Comstock imprint. In this decade, the press published the first of twenty-one volumes of the Cornell Wordsworth series and the first edition of Diana Sammataro's and Alphonse Avitabile's popular *Beekeeper's Handbook*.

The process of editing these and many other books was ably led for twenty-one years by Elsie Myers Stainton, who set a high standard as managing editor that continues to this day. After her retirement in 1976, Stainton published a series of books and articles about writing and editing, including the highly praised *The Fine Art of Copyediting*.

At the start of the 1970s, the press was a profitable and growing business, but Howley saw trouble on the horizon in the increasing costs of printing, promotion, editing, and general overhead. Increasing costs led to higher-priced books. In addition, university libraries, a key market for scholarly texts, were working with smaller budgets. In an interview, Howley said that "our books have long since been priced out of the reach of what should be our natural market—young scholars and students." To counter this, the press continued its tradition of publishing affordable paperbacks of titles with trade or course adoption potential, about 5 percent of its list and a total of 150 books since 1955.

The positive trends continued into the 1980s. In addition to maintaining the subsidiary office in London, the press had twenty sales representatives in contact with nearly one thousand retail stores across the country. Sales in Latin America were managed through UNILIBRO, a corporation operated by the presses at Cornell, Johns Hopkins, and Texas. A partnership with Phaidon Press of Oxford, UK, a publisher of art history books, was expanded to give Cornell University Press first North American rights to all Phaidon books. And a 1981 *Daily Sun* article reported an increase in books by and about women, particularly in literary criticism.

But the successes obscured deeper problems and the 1980s brought tumultuous times for the press, with several crises to navigate. In June 1982, a fire in a rented warehouse destroyed over 160,000 books valued at over half a million dollars. This disaster added to the financial difficulty already facing the press, precipitating a financial review by the university. Unlike most of the top university publishers, Cornell's press has never had an endowment to help it weather difficult times, though the university has made substantial contributions over the years to defray deficits and invest in improvements. Recommendations from the university included a comprehensive financial plan, closer oversight, and modernization of the press's practices.

Later that same year, Roger Howley left and Marilyn Sale, the managing editor, stepped in as interim director. This was an extremely difficult time for the press and it was largely through Sale's steady hand and intelligent leadership that staff confidence was restored as the press sought its new director. She was succeeded in 1983 by Walter Lippincott, who had been working as the press's acquisitions editor in New York City.

Lippincott arrived at a press with strong lists in the humanities—classics, literary criticism and theory, philosophy, music, and art history. The scholarly publishing landscape continued to pose challenges, and the press responded with tighter financial controls, an increased focus on acquiring the very best manuscripts, and an expansion into subject areas that might have an appeal beyond academia. Lippincott sought to strengthen the press's offerings in American history, Soviet studies, political science, agricultural and food policy, and certain scientific areas. The diversity of fields mirrored the broad mission of the university as both an arts and sciences institution and a land-grant school. The changes he implemented marked a turn to the editorial profile the press still maintains today.

Even during these difficult days, the press continued to publish many high-quality books, including *The National Question in Yugoslavia* by Ivo Banac, *Diseases of Trees and Shrubs* by Wayne Sinclair, Howard Lyon, and Warren Johnson, and *The Meaning of Nuclear Revolution* by Robert Jervis. The last won the first of six Grawemeyer Awards presented to Cornell authors over the next three decades, the most of any university press.

It was Lippincott who initiated the implementation of the first database at the warehouse, which gave the press the ability to undertake fulfillment and storage for other presses. With the energetic leadership of Dohn Barham, the chief financial officer, CUP Services (CUPS) expanded rapidly through the late 1980s and into the 1990s, diversifying the press's income stream at a crucial time. "The future of scholarly publishing is perilous," Lippincott admitted in a 1985 *Cornell Chronicle* article. But the university press is "absolutely essential for the publishing of quality scholarship. . . . It is here that we bring either credit or discredit to Cornell University."

Walter Lippincott, press director 1983–1986

Lippincott did much to turn the fortunes of the press around, though he stayed only until 1986, when he moved on to become director of the press at Princeton University, his alma mater. David Gilbert, who had been director of the University of Nebraska Press and associate director of the University of Texas Press, as well as a former president of AAUP, next took the helm. Through his hard work and knowledge of the publishing industry, he continued Lippincott's work of putting the press on more stable financial footing and increased the number of annual publications to over one hundred. Gilbert retired in 1989 and in an interview in the *Cornell Chronicle* left another ominous portent of the future of scholarly publishing. Citing the financial pressures on

David Gilbert, press director
1986–1989

John Ackerman, press director
1989–2014

libraries and publishers, plus the advent of new technologies, he predicted that "there are going to be big problems to solve in the next decade."

This challenging decade, in which library budgets continued to tighten and publishing costs to rise, was ushered in by the press's next director, John Ackerman. Ackerman had worked at the press since 1980, first as associate manuscript editor, then acquisitions editor in 1983, and editor in chief in 1985. His tenure brought a period of stability after the many difficulties of the 1980s—and some welcome changes.

The press continued to expand its lists in agriculture, the biological sciences, and the social sciences, with a political science list considered among the best in the nation, plus Ackerman's distinguished list in Soviet and Russian history. Executive Editor Roger Haydon, who came to the press in 1985, built a substantial list in Asian studies and played a crucial role in deepening and expanding the press's expertise in social and political science with two prominent series established by Lippincott, Cornell Studies in Political Economy and Cornell Studies in Security Affairs. New directions for the press included more feminist studies and African American studies—among them Isabel Hull's *Sexuality, State, and Civil Society in Germany, 1700–1815* and Charles Mills's *The Racial Contract*. In a *Cornell Chronicle* interview in 1991, Ackerman explained that part of Cornell's tradition was "to take what is at the forefront of research and bring it to the field where it can be applied practically." This, he continued, was the role of the press as well.

In the early 1990s, the press began looking for a new home that would be more functional and accessible than the three Roberts Place buildings. The search committee settled on Sage House, an elegant Victorian mansion located off campus. Once the home of Cornell trustee Henry Williams Sage and his wife, Susan Linn Sage, Sage House was designed by William Henry Miller, the architect of many important buildings on campus. Despite Henry Sage's numerous frustrations with the progress and quality of the construction, at its completion in 1880 he was very pleased by the elegant building with its bird-themed stained glass windows, fairytale fireplace tiles, and elaborate woodcarvings of owls, bats, and flowers. It was described in the local paper as looming up like a castle at the head of State Street and a "scene of rare beauty and magnificence."

After the death of Henry Sage in the late 1890s, the building was given to the university to be used as the student infirmary. The large dining room was converted into an X-ray room, a corner room on the second floor served as the operating room, and beds were installed throughout. It remained the university's infirmary, expanding into an extension wing, until the early 1980s. During those years, many students passed through what they nicknamed "the Morgue"—recuperating from the flu, having broken bones set after sledding accidents on the steep slope of nearby Buffalo Street, and suffering through the tragic typhoid epidemic of 1903 that filled the infirmary with nearly sixty patients.

Sage House officially became the new home of Cornell University Press in 1993. Like the old Roberts Place offices, it is an unconventional workplace with uneven heating, the occasional live bat, and rumored ghosts, but the staff loves it for its history and beauty.

In 1995, the press expanded in another new direction by merging with ILR Press. Cornell's Industrial and Labor Relations School began its publishing endeavors in 1948 under the unwieldy name of The Publishing Division of the New York State School of Industrial and Labor Relations at Cornell University, producing brochures, pamphlets, and books. The

ILR School and the press had worked together in the past on *ILR Review* (a separate entity) and produced some books, though the details of that arrangement are lost or buried deep in old file drawers. The long-time director of ILR's publishing division, Frances Benson, revitalized the press in the 1980s, shortening its name to the snappier ILR Press, broadening its scope by seeking authors outside Cornell, and building a reputation independent of the ILR School. ILR Press's publishing focus is labor, management, and the workplace, addressing issues that are relevant beyond the academic community and often anticipating trends, such as the role of women in the workplace in the 1970s and the culture of health care more recently.

Ackerman convinced Benson to stay on as the director of the new ILR Press imprint, and to become the editor in chief of Cornell University Press. The ILR imprint retained its editorial independence over book projects and its own editorial advisory board, an arrangement that continues to this day. In

Sage House, home of the press since 1993

2011, Benson was honored with an award from LERA (the Labor and Employment Relations Association) for the work she has done since the early 1970s to build ILR Press into a leading publisher of books on labor relations.

The century closed with one more innovation for the press, initiated by Design and Production Manager Deborah Bruner. In 1999, *A Living Wage,* by Lawrence Glickman, was the first book in the world to be printed on paper carrying the Forestry Stewardship Council logo, signifying that the trees harvested for the paper were grown using sustainable practices.

But the true end to this era of Cornell University Press could be said to have come a few years later, in 2004, when Acquisitions Editor Bernie Kendler retired after a remarkable forty-one years at the press, patiently prodding authors to produce their best work and teaching his coworkers by example. While the adoption of a database and newfangled desktop computers had hinted at the technology-infused world of publishing to come, it was Kendler's departure that in some ways marked the fading away of "traditional" university press publishing. New staff and new publishing realities were entering the scene to push the press into the digital age.

Early press logo

Digital Edition: Preparing for the Next 150 Years

The next transition of the press, from ink on paper to content in the cloud, has been one of halting first steps followed by rapid acceleration. Technology played an increasing role throughout the 1990s; at the time of the move to Sage House employees had desktop computers, but networks and a central server were seen by some (including the university's IT department) to be unnecessary and problematic. In 1995, recognizing the increasing importance of electronic data, the press implemented its first presswide database. People were still a bit hesitant about the use of new technology, however. The database committee report included an offhand remark that "electronic mail . . . is a hot item, and could offer some useful services to the press."

By the start of the new millennium, computers were the norm in every aspect of publishing; even the editing of manuscripts had changed from traditional pencil to electronic markup. As disruptive as these technological changes seemed at the time, however, they only hinted at the transformations to come. Staff members throughout the press embarked on steep learning curves that have continued to this day as the forms and procedures of publishing evolve at a brisk pace.

Mahinder Kingra and Peter Potter, interim press directors, 2014

The ongoing financial difficulties facing university presses, exacerbated first by the economic effects of the terrorist attacks of 9/11 and then by the Great Recession of 2007–9, necessitated experimentation with new publishing models. In 2010, the press, the Cornell University Library, and the Cornell German studies department collaborated to publish a German studies monograph series called Signale: Modern German Letters, Cultures, and Thoughts. With the aid of an Andrew W. Mellon Foundation grant, this series seeks to sustain quality, peer-reviewed academic research in an increasingly tough market by streamlining the publication process and reducing production costs through print-on-demand editions and e-books that are free to download in an open access model.

In the following year, the press began to issue the majority of its frontlist as e-books, as well as in print, embracing the changing technological landscape and seeking a remedy for the continued decline in print book sales. Budget-minded libraries increasingly moved toward purchasing digital books and journals. It was clear that e-books would play an ever larger role in the university press world and would require employees to learn new skills and the new terminology of digital assets and metadata.

No matter the form, the press continued to publish work by authors who were among the best in their fields. Books by Francis Fukuyama, P. W. Singer, Fiona Terry, Michael Barnett, and Suzanne Gordon won awards, sat prominently on bookshelves, and were downloaded onto Kindles. Executive Editor Roger Haydon has noted that the authors we publish, once entirely from Cornell, then from across the United States, are now increasingly from countries around the world, providing a broader perspective and alternative viewpoints in their research and writing. This growing global focus is also evident in the licensing of translations and other subsidiary rights to such far-flung and diverse countries as Thailand, Portugal, Croatia, Vietnam, China, and Georgia.

John Ackerman retired as director of the press in 2014. As an acquisitions editor, he left a legacy of many high-quality books and grateful authors who had benefited from his rigorous editing. As a director, he also left a press that had successfully made the first big steps into the world of e-books and print-on-demand, while maintaining the intellectual standards vital to the mission. Marketing Director Mahinder Kingra and Editor in Chief Peter Potter stepped in as interim codirectors, keeping the press running smoothly while the staff sought its new director over the next year.

In 2015, the press's current director, Dean Smith, arrived from Project MUSE at Johns Hopkins University Press, where he had served as director since 2010. The changes the press had begun to make in the previous decade to address the dramatic changes in the publishing world quickly kicked into high gear. Over the course of a year, the press implemented a new press-wide database, moved to a new royalties management system, changed its e-book distributor, and moved its book distribution

Dean J. Smith, press director
since 2015

to an outside warehouse, although this last step sadly meant
the closure of the press's own warehouse. Over time, consoli-
dation across the publishing industry had made smaller distribution operations such as CUPS less competitive.

The press is currently expanding the number of books
it publishes each year to over 150 and is publishing many
of these as print-on-demand, as well as in e-book form. In
2017, it launched two new imprints: Three Hills, created by
Senior Editor Michael McGandy, is a regional trade imprint
for smart and popular books on the natural history, history,
arts, science, culture, and current events of New York State
and the Northeast. SEAP Publications came from Cornell's
Southeast Asia Program, part of the Mario Einaudi Center for
International Studies, and brings with it a prestigious backlist of books and the *Indonesia Journal*. The marketing department broke new ground in 2018 with an experimental—and
very successful—pay-what-you-want sale that was praised by
both authors and students. Other opportunities are being ex-
plored, with the Einaudi Center and other parts of the Cornell

community, to strengthen our ties to the university by offering our skills and expertise in publishing projects that have scholarly merit but do not follow the typical peer-review path.

Two other recent major undertakings include a large-scale digitization of the press's extensive backlist and the creation of a collection of open access e-books. With the aid of grants from the National Endowment for the Humanities and the Mellon Foundation, Cornell Open was launched in 2017, bringing back classic titles in the humanities and sciences that had not been readily available for years. With the encouragement of the Cornell University Library, the press will continue to explore the possibilities of open access as a publishing model for both new and old books.

Many of these new strategies, while looking to the future, also reflect the mission-driven origins of the press. Providing publishing expertise to the Cornell community hearkens back to the earliest days when the press was dedicated solely to printing works for the university. The regional focus of the Three Hills imprint serves as a reminder of the numerous books published in the 1940s and 1950s about Cornell and New York State. And providing classic texts for free as downloadable e-books is a move that the Comstocks and Simon Gage, with their emphasis on affordable texts for students, would surely appreciate. The Comstock imprint itself is taking a new look at the idea of nature study and what it means in today's digital world, where concern about the media-driven disconnect from our natural surroundings parallels the effects of mass urbanization in the late nineteenth-century. Even the digitization of the backlist brings the rich history of the press out of dusty archives and gives it new life.

It was A. D. White's vision for the diffusion of new learning and Ezra Cornell's advocacy for making higher education available to all that gave rise to America's first university press. It was the support of key members of the university and the belief of the founders of Comstock Publishing in affordable, practical books that kept the idea of a university press at Cornell alive. And it has been the hard work of decades of dedicated staff members that has produced the many fine books by distinguished authors from Cornell and beyond—bringing the results of worthy scholarship to the world. The past 150 years have not been without struggle, sometimes seemingly insurmountable, but they have revealed a press that has been innovative from the start and that continues to adapt and change as the world changes. With the strength of this tradition behind it, Cornell University Press looks forward its next 150 years.

The editorial, design, and production departments review schedules for the week ahead, 2018. From left, Susan Specter, Ange Romeo-Hall, Sara Ferguson, Bill Oates, and Richie Patrick.

A Tradition of Excellence in 150 Notable Books

In celebration of the 150th anniversary of our founding, Cornell University Press presents 150 of our most notable books. These are bestsellers and award winners, books written by distinguished authors and that have made particularly important contributions to their fields—as well as books that are beloved by the staff or are important records of Cornell history. Drawing from close to 7,000 publications, our selections span the broad range of humanities and science fields in which we have published and reflect just a fraction of the important works and authors we have been proud to bring to the world.

1869   *Cornell University Register*

1888   John Henry Comstock, *An Introduction to Entomology*

1893   John Henry Comstock and Simon Henry Gage, eds., *Wilder Quarter-Century Book: A Collection of Original Papers Dedicated to Professor Burt Green Wilder*

1894   Simon Gage, *The Microscope*

1911   Anna Botsford Comstock, *Handbook of Nature-Study for Teachers and Parents*

1922   John Henry Comstock and William Gould Vinal, *Field and Camp Notebook*

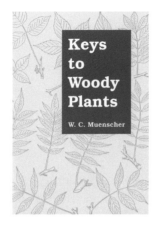

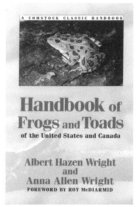

1949   Moses Coit Tyler, *A History of American Literature, 1607–1765*

1950   Walter Gellhorn, *Security, Loyalty, and Science*

1950   Karl von Frisch, *Bees: Their Vision, Chemical Senses, and Language*

1952   George Lenczowski, *The Middle East in World Affairs*

1954   Max Black, *Problems of Analysis: Philosophical Essays*

1954   Milton R. Konvitz, ed., *Bill of Rights Reader: Leading Constitutional Cases*

1954   Harry M. Orlinsky, *Ancient Israel*

1955   E. Harris Harbison, *The Age of Reformation*

1955   Ralph Vaughan Williams, *The Making of Music*

1956   R. E. Snodgrass, *Anatomy of the Honey Bee*

1957   G. E. M. Anscombe, *Intention*

1957   Charles Homer Haskins, *The Rise of Universities*

1958   Cadwallader Colden, *The History of the Five Indian Nations Depending on the Province of New-York in America*

1960   Clinton Rossiter, *Parties and Politics in America*

1961   Henry Guerlac, *Lavoisier: The Crucial Year: The Background and Origin of His First Experiments on Combustion in 1772*

1962   Morris Bishop, *A History of Cornell*

1962   Heinz Politzer, *Franz Kafka: Parable and Paradox*

1963   Walter Lafeber, *The New Empire: An Interpretation of American Expansion, 1860–1898*

1964   Angus Fletcher, *Allegory: The Theory of a Symbolic Mode*

1965   A. R. Ammons, *Tape for the Turn of the Year*

1966   David Brion Davis, *The Problem of Slavery in Western Culture*

1967   Claire Holt, *Art in Indonesia: Continuities and Change*

1967   Alvin Plantinga, *God and Other Minds: A Study of the Rational Justification of Belief in God*

1967   Victor Turner, *The Forest of Symbols: Aspects of Ndembu Ritual*

1968   Giambattista Vico, *The New Science of Giambattista Vico: Unabridged Translation of the Third Edition (1744)*, translated by Thomas Goddard Bergin and Max Harold Fisch

1969   Donald Kagan, *A New History of the Peloponnesian War* (4 vols.)

1970   Victor Shklovsky, *A Sentimental Journey: Memoirs, 1917–1922*

1971   Joseph Ḥayyim Brenner, *Breakdown and Bereavement: A Novel*, translated from the Hebrew by Hillel Halkin

1971   George Gibian, trans. and ed., *Russia's Literature of the Absurd: A Literary Discovery. Selected Works of Daniil Kharms and Alexander Vvedensky*

1971   Georg Henrik von Wright, *Explanation and Understanding*

1971   Mack Walker, *German Home Towns: Community, State, and General Estate, 1648–1871*

1972   Jeffrey Burton Russell, *Witchcraft in the Middle Ages*

1972   Carl Sagan and Thornton Page, eds., *UFO's: A Scientific Debate*

1973   Diana Sammataro and Alphonse Avitabile, *The Beekeeper's Handbook*

1974   Barbara G. Myerhof, *Peyote Hunt: The Sacred Journey of the Huichol Indians*

1975–2007   William Wordsworth, *The Cornell Wordsworth* (21 vols.)

1977   Marquis de Lafayette, *Lafayette in the Age of the American Revolution: Selected Letters and Papers, 1776–1790*, edited by Stanley J. Idzerda, Roger E. Smith, Linda J. Pike, Mary Ann Quinn, and Robert R. Crout (5 vols.)

1977   Norman Malcolm, *Memory and Mind*

1978   Seymour Chatman, *Story and Discourse: Narrative Structure in Fiction and Film*

1978   William Murphy, *Prodigal Father: The Life of John Butler Yeats (1839–1922)*

1980   Nina Baym, *Woman's Fiction: A Guide to Novels by and about Women in America, 1820–1870*

1980   William R. Biers, *The Archaeology of Greece: An Introduction*

1980   Harold Bloom, *Wallace Stevens: The Poems of Our Climate*

1980   Michael Kammen, ed., *The Past before Us: Contemporary Historical Writing in the United States*

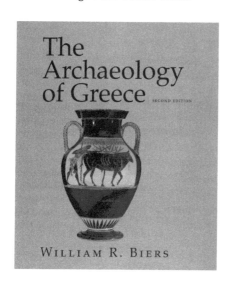

1980   Merritt Roe Smith, *Harpers Ferry Armory and the New Technology: The Challenge of Change*

1981   Whitney R. Cross, *Burned-over District: The Social and Intellectual History of Enthusiastic Religion in Western New York, 1800–1850*

1981   Fredric Jameson, *The Political Unconscious: Narrative as a Socially Symbolic Act*

1982–2013   William Butler Yeats, *The Cornell Yeats* (33 vols.)

1982   Jonathan Culler, *On Deconstruction: Theory and Criticism after Structuralism*

1982   Geoffrey E. Maurice Ste. Croix, *The Class Struggle in the Ancient Greek World: From the Archaic Age to the Arab Conquests*

1983   Dominick LaCapra, *Rethinking Intellectual History: Texts, Contexts, Language*

1984   Ivo Banac, *The National Question in Yugoslavia: Origins, History, Politics*

1984   Plato and Aristophanes, *Four Texts on Socrates: Plato's "Euthyphro," "Apology," and "Crito" and Aristophanes' "Clouds,"* translated with notes by Thomas G. West and Grace Starry West, introduction by Thomas G. West

1985   Luce Irigaray, *Speculum of the Other Woman*

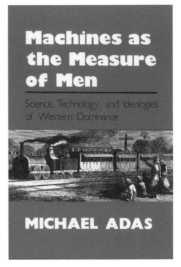

1985   Peter Katzenstein, *Small States in World Markets: Industrial Policy in Europe*

1985   Nancy B. Reich, *Clara Schumann: The Artist and the Woman*

1986   Jack Flam, *Matisse: The Man and His Art, 1869–1918*

1986   Elliot J. Gorn, *The Manly Art: Bare-Knuckle Prize Fighting in America*

1986   Sandra Harding, *The Science Question in Feminism*

1987   Charles Darwin, *Charles Darwin's Notebooks 1836–1844: Geology, Transmutation of Species, Metaphysical Enquiries*, transcribed and edited by Paul H. Barrett, Peter J. Gautrey, Sandra Herbert, David Kohn, and Sydney Smith

1987   Wayne A. Sinclair, Howard H. Lyon, and Warren T. Johnson, *Diseases of Trees and Shrubs*

1988   P. V. Glob, *The Bog People: Iron-Age Man Preserved*

1989   Jack Donnelly, *Universal Human Rights in Theory and Practice*

1989   Robert Jervis, *The Meaning of Nuclear Revolution: Statecraft and the Prospect of Armageddon*

1989   Barbara Kingsolver, *Holding the Line: Women in the Great Arizona Mine Strike of 1983*

1989   Alexander F. Skutch, *Life of the Tanager*, illustrated by Dana Gardner

1989   Gary Stiles and Alexander F. Skutch, *A Guide to the Birds of Costa Rica*, illustrated by Dana Gardner

1990   Michael Adas, *Machines as the Measure of Men: Science, Technology, and Ideologies of Western Dominance*

1990   Benedict Anderson, *Language and Power: Exploring Political Cultures in Indonesia*

1990   Robert V. Bruce, *Bell: Alexander Graham Bell and the Conquest of Solitude*

1990   Peter Kivy, *Music Alone: Philosophical Reflections on the Purely Musical Experience*

1990   Gregory Nagy, *Greek Mythology and Poetics*

1991   William P. Alston, *Perceiving God: The Epistemology of Religious Experience*

1991   Peter Uwe Hohendahl, *Reappraisals: Shifting Alignments in Postwar Critical Theory*

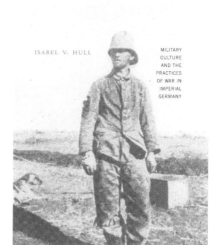

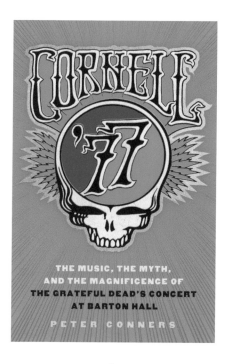

Acknowledgments

Researching and writing the history of the press has been a labor of love over several years, and one that could not have been completed without the help of many other people. I am grateful to John Ackerman, Fran Benson, and Roger Haydon for passing historical documents and books into my care and telling me stories about the press that stretch back over forty years. I offer a belated thank you to the employees of our now-closed warehouse for carefully maintaining our historical archive of books, enabling me to piece together our early publishing history. I thank John Ackerman again, plus Bernie Kendler and many current staff members of the press, for helping me compile a list of notable books, though I apologize for the many excellent suggestions I had to leave out. In addition, I am grateful to Evan Fay Earle and Laura Linke of the Cornell University Library Rare and Manuscript Collection for guiding me through the archival research. Finally, I thank the other members of the press history subcommittee—Jonathan Hall, Ellen Murphy, Richie Patrick, Jennifer Savran Kelly, and James McCaffery (plus all the other coworkers I managed to rope in for particular tasks)—for helping me with research, with the process of putting this book together, and with preparing all the blog, Facebook, and Instagram posts that are a requisite part of any modern publishing endeavor.

The beautiful design of this book was created by retired press designer Lou Robinson and pays tribute to the work of William Henry Miller, the architect of Sage House, in its use of photos of architectural elements of the building. Scott Levine, art director, was generous with his limited free time in taking these photos and others.

—Karen M. Laun

Bibliographical Note

The initial sources for the history of Cornell University Press and Comstock Publishing were found in the Cornell University Press archives, including previously written histories. The Cornell University Library Rare and Manuscript Collection was a vital source of historical photographs, biographical files on early directors, and information on the building of Sage House. Digitized primary sources at the university and elsewhere made research a much easier task than in decades past and the following sources were invaluable: Cornell University Board of Trustees reports, annual reports of the president of Cornell University, *Ithaca Daily Journal*, *Ithaca Journal*, *Cornell Alumni News*, *Cornell Bulletin*, *Cornell Chronicle*, *Cornell Daily Sun*, *Cornell Era*, *Cornell Magazine*, *Cornell Register*, and *Cornell Plantations* magazine.

The history of Comstock Publishing is detailed in an unpublished 1944 manuscript, "A Half-Century of the Comstock Publishing Company; 1893–1943," by Simon Henry Gage and Clara Starrett Gage. Accounts of the early history of Cornell University Press were found in a draft chapter by Woodford Patterson for Robert Frederick Lane, "The Place of American University Presses in Publishing" (PhD diss., University of

Chicago, 1938) and in B. Alsterlund and Walter Pilkington, "The First Real University Press in the United States," *American Notes and Queries* (August 1946). The best and most enjoyable source for the history of Cornell in general is always Morris Bishop's *A History of Cornell* (Ithaca: Cornell University Press, 1962).

Roaming farther afield, sources include J. M. Hart, "Cornell University," *Scribner's Monthly* (May 1873); John H. Selkreg, ed., *Landmarks of Tompkins County* (Syracuse: D. Mason & Company, 1894); Peter Givler, "University Press Publishing in the United States," http://www.aupresses.org/about-aaup/about-university-presses/history-of-university-presses; John K. Hutchens, "One Thing and Another," *Saturday Review* (June 21, 1969); and Morris Bishop, "The Lower Depths of Higher Education," *American Heritage* 21, 1 (1969).

Photo Credits

Photos of Ezra Cornell, A. D. White, Daniel Willard Fiske, Morrill Hall, George Lincoln Burr, Sibley College, John Henry Comstock, Simon Henry Gage, Anna Botsford Comstock, Lane Cooper, Woodford Patterson, Victor Reynolds, Roger Howley, David Gilbert, and John Ackerman are printed here courtesy of the Cornell University Library Rare and Manuscript Collection. Walter Lippincott, Mahinder Kingra, and Peter Potter kindly provided photos of themselves. The present-day photos of Cornell staff and of Sage House architecture are courtesy of Scott Levine. All other photos are property of the press.

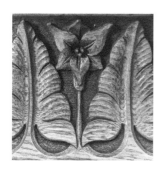

The People behind the Books

Director's Office

Dean J. Smith, *Director*
Michael A. Morris, *Assistant to the Director and Building Coordinator*

Acquisitions

Mahinder Kingra, *Editor in Chief*
Emily Andrew, *Senior Editor*
Frances Benson, *Editorial Director, ILR Press*
Sarah E. M. Grossman, *Managing Editor, SEAP Publications*
Roger Haydon, *Executive Editor*
James Lance, *Senior Editor*
Kitty Liu, *Editor, Comstock Publishing Associates*
Michael J. McGandy, *Senior Editor and Editorial Director, Three Hills*
Bethany Wasik, *Assistant Editor*
Meagan Dermody, *Acquisitions Assistant*
Ellen F. Murphy, *Acquisitions Assistant*

Subsidiary Rights and Permissions

Tonya Cook, *Subsidiary Rights Manager*
Stephanie Munson, *Permissions Coordinator*

Manuscript Editing

Ange Romeo-Hall, *Managing Editor*
Sara Ferguson, *Production Editor*
Karen Hwa, *Senior Production Editor*
Jennifer Savran Kelly, *Production Editor*
Karen M. Laun, *Senior Production Editor and Digital Publishing Editor*
Susan Specter, *Senior Production Editor*
James McCaffery, *Digital Publishing Assistant*

Design and Production

Scott Levine, *Art Director*
Richanna Patrick, *Designer and Apple IT*
Diana R. Silva, *Senior Production Coordinator*
Bill Oates, *Production Coordinator*

Marketing and Sales

Martyn Beeny, *Marketing and Sales Director*
Adriana M. Ferreira, *Social Media Coordinator*
Nathan D. Gemignani, *Special Sales Representative and Metadata*
Carmen Torrado Gonzalez, *Marketing Assistant*
Jonathan L. Hall, *Digital Marketing Manager*
David Mitchell, *Exhibits, Advertising, and Awards Coordinator*
Cheryl Quimba, *Publicity Manager*

Business Office

Lynn A. Benedetto, *Finance and Royalty Manager*
William O'Dell Wehling, *Accounts Representative*
Kate Leboff, *Project Manager*

Information Technology

Patrick Garrison, *CIS Computing Manager and IT Administrator*

Our Sponsor

We thank Apex CoVantage for their
continued generosity and exemplary
service in publishing this book and
many others in over ten years of
successful partnership.